BUSINI
NETWORKING
FOR STARTUPS AND
SIDE HUSTLERS

How to Build a Profitable Business
Network Fast!

Anthony Lindsay - CeMaP, CeReR

Business Networking For Startups and Side Hustlers

Strategic Networking for Startup Success and

Side Hustle Growth

Anthony Lindsay - CeMaP, CeReR

Before you get started be sure to access our Networking GPT. It will take your networking to another level!

Table Of Contents

Acknowledgement

To claim I've got it all figured out would be far from the truth. But after more than five decades on this earth, I've come to realize that a significant part of life hinges on pattern recognition. This knack for discerning patterns has been sharpened over years spent with my nose in various business books. As I've navigated my entrepreneurial path, the wisdom gleaned from these pages has helped me arrange my actions into sequences that breed productivity and efficiency.

This book is a salute to every author whose work has guided me and to those whose books I've yet to explore. As the adage goes, "You will be the same person next year as you are today, except for the books you read and the people you meet." It's in this spirit that I underscore the value of networking—it's not just about business growth; it's about personal evolution.

So, this acknowledgment extends beyond a simple 'thank you.' It's an affirmation that the knowledge shared by others is what propels us forward, and for that, I am eternally grateful. Let this book serve as a continuation of that tradition of sharing knowledge, and may it enrich your life as much as others' works have enriched mine.

This book is perfect for anyone who wants to learn how to network better. I will reference a few networking organizations. It would be impossible for me to know about every networking group that exists so I will focus on the ones that I have been a member of or have proven to be worth knowing.

Now that you are part of my network please feel free to share information about other organizations that our readers would benefit from joining.

Opening Comments

When I decided to take my business to the next level, I knew that effective networking would be crucial. I set a goal to attend at least one networking event each week, a habit that's become a cornerstone of my professional growth. Over time, people began to ask me how to transform networking efforts into something genuinely productive. While success is subjective, most would concur that creating tangible business opportunities is a hallmark of successful networking.

But there's more to it than just business transactions. The true essence of networking lies in forging authentic connections, not merely transactional ones where every conversation is a veiled sales pitch. This book is about striking that delicate balance—building relationships that are both genuine and professionally beneficial. It's about what to do, and just as importantly, what not to do, as you navigate the networking landscape.

As a business owner, networking is not an activity relegated to specific events; it's a continuous process. Every day presents a new opportunity to meet someone new and to broaden your horizon. Whether you're at the grocery store, attending a seminar, or even during a casual social gathering, every interaction is a chance to learn and expand your network.

Let this book be your guide to cultivating a network that grows with you and supports your business journey. By being a consistent networker you will always have access to the people and information that you need before you need it. I find that often, business owners have no interest in networking until they need something and then it's too late.

A quick tip for Linkedin Networking. It takes time to build a meaningful network so dedicate some time each week to comment on posts and generate content that people will find informative.

Poor Planning

As we move from the foundational mindset that underpins successful networking, laid out in the acknowledgment of the power of pattern recognition, we turn to a more tactical aspect: planning. Without a strategy, networking is just socializing without a purpose. And while socializing has its place, as entrepreneurs and go-getters, we are on a mission.

Poor planning is the Achilles' heel of networking. Entering an event without a clear objective is akin to setting sail without a compass. What we measure we can manage, so have an idea of how many new people you want to meet.

Networking should be an integral part of your business strategy, a structured approach to forging new relationships, finding customers, creating synergies, and broadcasting your brand. Success in networking hinges on your clarity of purpose—knowing what success looks like for you. This could mean making one new contact that you know you will build a productive relationship with.

Arriving early at events can work to your advantage. It's in these quiet moments before the crowd swells that the seeds of fruitful partnerships are often sown. Picture this: you could be offering a word of encouragement to the event organizer, who's likely a bundle of nerves, counting the early attendees. Having been in their shoes, organizing conferences and expos myself, I can attest that we're appreciative and more open to conversation with the early birds.

Don't leave your house without a stack of business cards or promotional materials. Yes, despite our digital age, business cards remain a tangible token of professionalism and preparedness. They can set you apart in a crowd increasingly reliant on digital connections. And a word to the wise: if your business card or materials point people to your website, make doubly sure it's operational. There's little worse in our digital world than a potential contact being greeted with a 404 error. This will be covered later on in this book.

Networking Tip of the Topic!

Transform Your Business Card into a Coupon or Call to Action

Let's take a page from the playbook of the brilliant Bill Walsh, whom I had the pleasure of meeting a few years back. Currently, your business card might be a modest piece of cardstock that lists your contact information. But here's a powerful tweak: turn it into a coupon or a sales pitch.

Utilize the real estate on the back of the card to extend an exclusive offer or compelling pitch. This not only makes your card memorable but also adds value for the recipient, increasing the likelihood they'll hold onto it—and more importantly, reach out to you.

Action Plan To Plan Better

Specific: Prepare for networking events by setting clear goals, arriving early, and ensuring an adequate supply of business cards and functional promotional materials.

Measurable: Success can be measured by the number of meaningful conversations initiated, business cards distributed, and follow-ups planned.

Achievable: By dedicating time to pre-event preparation, including website checks and material readiness, these goals are within reach.

Relevant: These actions are directly tied to maximizing the impact of networking opportunities.

Time-Bound: Before each networking event, allocate at least one hour for strategic planning and preparation.

The Follow-Up Factor: Converting Contacts into Opportunities

Another barrier to successful networking is not being prepared for the follow-up or delivery. Reflect on this: a study by the Association for Sales Executives revealed that 81% of all sales happen on or after the fifth contact. Yet, the same study found that 90% of people do not follow up with a contact more than three times. This gap signifies a massive opportunity for those who are diligent with their follow-up strategy.

Consider a large networking event I attended in New York, where I met dozens of people. To capitalize on this, I had already set up a lead funnel in my CRM, programmed to send automated follow-up emails to each new contact within 48 hours—timing is crucial, as another report suggests that following up within an hour of meeting can make you seven times more likely to have a meaningful conversation with decision-makers.

I crafted a simple yet effective funnel, incorporating details of our discussions, ensuring personalized follow-up communication. It also reminded me to make a phone call, reinforcing that personal touch that's so often lost in the digital shuffle. The lesson is simple: while meeting people is foundational, following up in a timely manner is where the transformative interactions occur.

In my decades of experience organizing conferences in Houston, New York, Birmingham, and London, I've often been asked, "How many people are you expecting?" This question, while important, pales compared to considering how many connections you can realistically engage with in a meaningful way. If you met 30 potential customers or business partners, what would your process be? How would you manage that data? Do you have the capacity to deliver on what you say you do? If the answer is uncertain, then it's crucial to reassess your approach.

Remember, timely follow-up is not just a nicety—it's a business necessity. In a survey by InTouch, they found that 48% of people never even make a single follow-up attempt. This means that by simply reaching out for a second contact, you're already ahead of half the competition.

Equip yourself with a strategy that doesn't just collect business cards, but one that turns those cards into lasting and productive relationships.

Follow-up Tip of the Topic

To elevate your startup or side hustle, a Customer Relationship Management (CRM) system isn't just beneficial; it's a must-have. Once you have a CRM in place, leverage it by building a simple yet effective 'networking' sales funnel. Here's how you can set it up:

Immediate Engagement: As soon as you've entered a new contact into your CRM, trigger an automated "It was nice meeting you" email. This initial touchpoint keeps the connection warm and shows you value the interaction.

Personal Reminder: Use your CRM to set a personal reminder to call them. A phone call adds a human element that emails can't replicate, setting the stage for a stronger relationship.

Follow-Up Interaction: After your call, invite them to a brief follow-up call or meeting to discuss potential synergies. This step cements the intention to pursue a professional relationship.

Crucially, make sure to record at least one unique detail about the person or your conversation in the CRM. This personalized touch can make all the difference; it helps them remember you amidst a sea of contacts and equally helps you recall them, laying the groundwork for a conversation that continues naturally from where you left off.

Remember, successful networking is about consistency and personalization. Use your CRM to ensure no valuable new connection falls through the cracks, this will help avoid data leakage.

Here is an example of how to make your networking effective:

Last night, I attended a networking event where I met a young woman who works for HUB.tv. She mentioned that they were hosting a contest in search of someone with an innovative product. The winner would receive $20,000, national marketing exposure, a trip to China, and features on major television programs.

Although this opportunity wasn't relevant for me—I don't have any products that fit the criteria—I knew several people I met that night who did. I made sure to connect these individuals with the opportunity.

While nothing might come of it, my past experiences suggest that those people will remember the gesture.

Be A Giver, Don't be Selfish With Contacts

In my opinion, being selfish with contacts is the primary reason why networking fails. We must remember, "We can all eat!" There's no need to worry that sharing someone's information or connecting two people will result in lost business. In fact, studies show that professionals who actively share their network are 58% more likely to have increased business opportunities. Yet, I observe many individuals who attend networking events, gather numerous business cards, but never strategize on how to connect these new contacts with their existing network. This is a misstep!

I do the exact opposite, both at events and afterward. I moderate a few WhatsApp groups for this very reason. When I meet someone who I believe would be a valuable contact for others in my network, I invite them to join my WhatsApp group, pointing out individuals I think they would benefit from knowing. I then reach out to those existing contacts and let them know I have someone I'd like them to meet. This method is efficient because it's handled within the group, and everyone benefits.

Adopting this method has increased my value within my network; people see me as a resourceful contact for networking and finding business opportunities. The laws of reciprocity are at play here—they just work. The key is to be organized and pragmatic about your networking approach.

Another tip for LinkedIn, when you make a post, don't be afraid jumpstart the conversation by being the first to comment. Once people react to your posts be sure to thank them, it will encourage them to comment on your future posts.

Being a Connector Tip of the Topic

Don't just collect contacts; be the bridge that connects them. Each person you meet has the potential to benefit others in your network. Actively introduce new contacts to those you already know who may have mutual interests or complementary needs.

Create a Networking Group: Whether it's on WhatsApp, LinkedIn, or any other platform, create a group dedicated to professional networking within your industry or interest area.

Personalize Introductions: When adding someone new, give a brief introduction that includes how and why you think they'd be a valuable addition. Mention specific individuals they should connect with and why.

Follow-Up: After making an introduction, check in with both parties to see if they've connected and offer any further assistance in fostering the relationship.

Remember, by helping others connect, you position yourself as a valuable and influential figure in your network.

This not only increases your own business prospects through the law of reciprocity but also strengthens the entire network, creating a community of support and opportunity.

If you decide to start a Whatsapp group you should find a few people to help you build and manage the group. In my experience it is best to set clear rules for the group.

In my groups I ask that people only post once per week to avoid the group becoming 'spammy'. The worst thing that can happen is for people to put the chat on mute. It is better to have a few engaged people than hundreds of people with the group on mute.

Your Global Store Front Sucks!

In the previous chapter, we uncovered the power of networking through the act of connecting others. Now, let's turn our attention to another crucial touchpoint that often serves as the first impression of your brand: your website.

Your website is your global storefront, and frankly, for many I've encountered in recent networking events, it sucks! There's no gentle way to put this. A staggering 40% of the professionals I've met in the past three months were underselling themselves, and here are the top three reasons why their websites were failing them:

The "Eternal Construction" Site: A website perpetually under construction (for the past eight months, no less) is a testament to procrastination or neglect, neither of which reflects well on your business.

The Attention Repellent: Websites that are poorly designed fail to capture attention, let alone retain it. If your site looks like it belongs in the early 2020s, it's time for a facelift.

The Link Graveyard: Broken links and missing images are the digital equivalent of cracked windows and a "Closed" sign. They drive potential customers away.

In our interconnected world, there's absolutely no excuse for not having a sleek, functional website. With the plethora of free, affordable, and user-friendly web design options available, creating an online presence that makes you look good should be non-negotiable.

Let's explore how you can turn your website from a business liability into a powerful asset.

Website Tip of The Topic

If your website isn't up to par or still in the digital equivalent of an "under construction" phase, pivot to your social media platforms. LinkedIn, for example, can serve as your interim online business card.

Profile Makeover: Ensure your LinkedIn profile has a professional photo and a relevant, eye-catching header image.

Content Refresh: Update all sections of your LinkedIn or social media profiles with the latest information about your professional experience, skills, and accomplishments.

Link Smart: If your website isn't ready for visitors, include a link on your social media profile to an alternative online space that showcases your work, such as a digital portfolio, blog, or even a more polished social media page.

Remember, your social media profiles are often the first-place new contacts will go to learn more about you. Make sure they encounter the best version of your digital presence, one that's current, compelling, and free of the dreaded "under construction" banner or broken links.

Bonus Social Media Tip

Take your networking game to the next level by leveraging a personal QR code that links directly to your LinkedIn page or another social media profile.

Action Steps:

Generate Your QR Code: Use a free online QR code generator to create a code that links directly to your professional social media page.

Display with Pride: Add your QR code to your business card, event nametag, or even your presentation slides.

Instant Connection: At networking events, invite new contacts to scan your QR code. It's a modern, quick, and touch-free way to connect on the spot.

This small but mighty tool can revolutionize the way you exchange information. It's efficient, eco-friendly, and ensures that your new contacts have instant access to your digital presence. Plus, it positions you as a tech-savvy professional. Go ahead, give it a try—you can thank me later!

A Quick Reminder Of Who Not To Be

Avoid being a 'Greedy Gretchen' or 'Greedy Gary' – While I've never personally encountered Gretchen or Gary, their reputations precede them. They're known for dominating conversations, incessantly talking about themselves without showing any interest in others. They're pushy, rarely asking questions that invite dialogue, and the most irksome trait? Their lack of eye contact. It's said they constantly scan the room, treating the person they're speaking AT as nothing more than a placeholder until someone more 'important' comes along.

The takeaway here is simple: don't be greedy. Be generous with your attention. Stay present in the conversation. Take the opportunity to learn about the person you're engaging with.

Another Linkedin tip. Don't make your first contact with a new connection a sales pitch. Build a relationship before pushing your products and services.

Beyond the Business Card: Cultivating Lasting Connections

Ok, so you've been to a fantastic networking event. You've made some solid connections, and they're all neatly entered into your CRM. You've even scheduled a time for a short follow-up chat—this is where true networking really begins. Like most, you might not have a clear plan for what to do or say next. But don't worry, I've got your back.

Your next move is to really get to know the person and understand what they need for their business. Why were they at the networking event in the first place? What's their business about? The goal here is to listen—really listen. If networking doesn't come naturally to you, consider preparing a few thoughtful questions beforehand. The aim of this initial conversation is to dive deep into understanding who you're talking to.

You might discover common professional interests or even personal ones. Use this first interaction as an opportunity to uncover their business needs and pain points. Remember to be genuine. There's no room for hidden agendas here. Yes, you have goals—networking is, after all, a two-way street—but your agenda should be transparent. It's about finding that intersection where both of your needs can meet and benefit mutually.

Tip Of The Topic

Follow up after an event by setting clear parameters and objectives.

Set a Time Limit: Keep the first meeting concise—aim for 15-20 minutes. This respects both parties' time and keeps the conversation focused.

Prepare Open-Ended Questions: Develop at least three open-ended questions that encourage dialogue and deeper understanding. For example.

- "What inspired you to start your business, and what are you aiming to achieve in the next year?"

- "Can you tell me about a challenge you've recently faced in your industry, and how you're navigating it?"

- "What value do you believe your business brings to clients, and what makes it stand out?"

Active Listening: Use this time to actively listen and engage with their responses. This will help you identify areas where you may be able to offer assistance or collaboration.

Be Transparent with Your Intentions: As you discuss, be upfront about your networking goals. If there's a potential for collaboration or mutual benefit, let them know you're interested in exploring those possibilities.

By limiting the initial meeting time and asking targeted, open-ended questions, you create an environment conducive to building a connection. This structure ensures you both leave the meeting with a clear understanding of the potential for future interactions.

Adding Value, Why I love AppSumo

Once you've peeled back the initial layer and learned more about your new acquaintance's business interests, it's time to consider how you can be of value to them. This doesn't necessarily mean a grand gesture. Sometimes, it's as simple as passing on a contact from your own network or recommending a resource that has been instrumental in your success.

Consider this: according to a study by the American Marketing Association, customers who are the recipients of a firm's generosity, such as free advice or referrals, can increase sales referrals by as much as 107%. The act of adding value is potent, and it's foundational for building strong professional relationships.

For me, AppSumo has been a treasure trove for such resources. It's a marketplace for new and innovative apps offering what they call 'lifetime offers.' You make one purchase and have access to the app indefinitely, which is backed by a 30-day money-back guarantee. My business and the insights I share in this book are largely powered by tools I've acquired through AppSumo.

And here's why this is important for you: If you stumble upon a find on AppSumo that enhances your efficiency or saves costs, you'll likely remember where you got the tip from and value this book even more. Now, imagine sharing a similar resource with a new contact after your initial meeting. If that resource helps them save or earn money, how do you think they will view you?

This is where the law of reciprocity kicks in—a social norm suggesting people tend to return a favor. By sharing valuable information or resources, you're not only helping someone out, but you're also laying the groundwork for a reciprocal relationship.

This could mean new opportunities and valuable insights coming your way, effectively giving you a return on your investment of time, and creating a solid foundation for a fruitful business relationship.

Smart Sourcing with AppSumo Tip Of The Topic

For every business owner, time and money are the twin pillars supporting the journey to success. The right business apps can reinforce both.

Explore AppSumo: Visit and browse through their extensive collection of business tools.

Select Wisely: Look for apps that address your current business needs—be it marketing, project management, or customer service.

Invest Smartly: Take advantage of AppSumo's lifetime offers to make a one-time purchase for ongoing utility.

Remember, the goal is to run a lean, efficient, and profitable operation. With AppSumo's resources, you're likely to find tools that can give you an edge. And when you do, it's not just a win for your business operations; it's a nod to your savvy as a business owner. Trust me, taking this step is likely to be one of those decisions you'll look back on with gratitude.

Establish Effective Networking Follow-Ups

Specific: Set up a system within your CRM for following up after networking events.

Measurable: Aim to follow up with at least 80% of the contacts you meet at each event.

Achievable: Utilize automated email triggers and set reminders for personal follow-up calls.

Relevant: Effective follow-ups are crucial for turning networking encounters into valuable business relationships.

Time-Bound: Implement this system for your next networking event and review its effectiveness monthly.

Enhance Online Presence with a Professional Website

Specific: Create or revamp your business website to be professional, user-friendly, and informative.

Measurable: The website should have zero broken links, a modern design, and updated content.

Achievable: Use platforms like WordPress, Wix, or work with a professional designer.

Relevant: A well-maintained website is essential for a credible online presence.

Time-Bound: Complete the website update or creation within the next three months.

Utilize AppSumo to Streamline Business Operations

Specific: Find and implement at least two new tools from AppSumo that can improve your business operations.

Measurable: Achieve a noticeable improvement in time management or cost reduction.

Achievable: Regularly explore AppSumo for relevant tools and read reviews to ensure they meet your business needs.

Relevant: Investing in efficient tools can significantly enhance productivity and profitability.

Time-Bound: Identify and integrate these tools within the next 60 days.

Investing in Your Network: The Power of Paid Networking Groups

I wasn't entirely sure where to place this chapter in the book, but I eventually decided to introduce it now. The reason being, until you've honed your networking skills and experienced some degree of success, the idea of investing in a networking group might not seem very appealing. However, once you've tasted even a modicum of success, the advantages of scaling up become much clearer.

At this juncture, the main challenge for you, especially as a startup or side hustler, might be limited funds (in the case of startups) or time constraints (for side hustlers). But, if you take my advice to heart, you'll find ways to make it work. Joining a structured networking group is essential, and I cannot emphasize enough the importance of being part of a group that requires a membership fee. Yes, you heard me right — pay to join.

I'll delve deeper into the reasoning behind this in the upcoming chapters and will also recommend some groups worth joining. So, please keep an open mind as we explore this further.

Before we continue, I must mention one of the inspirations for this book, Nick Davis. You can find him at www.linkedin.com/in/nicholasdavishouston. Nick was the president of my BNI group in Houston. Before he became President, he was a member who always brought energy to the group. Nick is an amazing person, always willing to help. If you google 'reclaim your premium,' you will find all his awesome content.

I mention Nick because he not only knows how to build a personal brand but also how to build meaningful relationships and connect people. The fact that he is a dynamic speaker means that he can do things that many cannot. However, the one thing we can all do is bring positive energy to every situation, which will always make your networking efforts more effective.

Why You Should Pay

When I suggest that you should pay to join a networking group, it's in addition to engaging in FREE networking groups and perhaps starting your own group on Facebook, WhatsApp, or any other easily managed platform. However, it's crucial to be part of a paid networking group for several reasons.

Firstly, the financial commitment will motivate you to be an active participant, a sentiment shared by other paying members. You'll often find that members of paid groups are of higher quality – they tend to be more serious, reliable, and driven. This is not just about spending money; it's about investing in a space where serious business owners and professionals gather.

Additionally, think of your membership fee as an investment in your business. Networking done right should be bringing in revenue. View these fees as part of your marketing budget; every business allocates funds to marketing, and networking is an essential aspect of it.

Lastly, paying for membership pushes you to be more focused and data driven. To justify the cost, you'll need to understand your customer's worth, your conversion rates, retention, customer lifetime value, referral value, and all those other 'boring' yet crucial numbers. This is where a good CRM comes into play, providing you with this data effortlessly.

I've been deliberate about the technical aspects to highlight how integral a business plan and a CRM are to your networking success. Yes, effective networking is deeply connected to both.

Now is also an ideal time to discuss the importance of investing in yourself and your business, as well as the significance of surrounding yourself with people who do the same. As a small business owner, I understand the necessity of being financially prudent. However, it's crucial to invest in yourself.

I recall attending an event where the organizer explained his rationale for not advertising on Gumtree. He said, 'Gumtree is where cheap people find cheap services.' This isn't meant to disparage Gumtree, but rather to emphasize the point: don't be frugal at the expense of your business's quality.

Investing in yourself involves both time and money, both of which are essential for building a solid foundation. Similarly, networking requires an investment of time and money.

Statistically speaking, a survey by the Small Business Administration reveals that businesses investing in quality marketing and personal development tend to experience a 15-20% higher growth rate compared to those that do not. Furthermore, a Forbes study shows that 70% of successful small business owners recognize the significant impact of strategic investments in personal and business areas on their overall success.

5 Free Business Networking Platforms

LinkedIn: A professional networking site that allows you to connect with other professionals, join industry groups, and participate in discussions.

Meetup: Offers a platform to join or create groups based on professional interests and attend local events or meetups.

Facebook Groups: Numerous industry-specific groups exist where professionals can network, share resources, and get advice.

Eventbrite: While primarily an event management site, it offers access to various free networking events and workshops.

Reddit: Subreddits like r/Entrepreneur, r/Startups, and r/small business provide platforms for advice, sharing experiences, and networking.

The Problem With Free Networks

The issue with free business networks, despite my recommendation to join a few, is that they often lack focus and moderation. In many instances, these groups consist of individuals primarily trying to sell their services or products, frequently disregarding the networking principles outlined in this book. This is not to say that there aren't valuable free networks out there, but because the barrier to entry is generally low, the quality can be inconsistent.

This often means that you could spend a substantial amount of time in these groups without seeing a meaningful return on your investment of time. However, the silver lining is that your CRM system will be invaluable in helping you track the productivity of these networks.

By monitoring your interactions and the outcomes, you can assess whether a particular group is worth your continued involvement.

Not to mention, the majority of these FREE networks operate online, which poses another challenge. The virtual nature of these platforms often means missing out on the opportunity to forge deeper, more meaningful relationships.

There's a certain dynamic and connection that comes from face-to-face interactions, which can be hard to replicate in an online setting.

Remember, the guidance in this book is just that, guidance. Only you know what will work best for you and your business. In most cases my advice is not binary. A mixture of strategies is what you should aim for.

5 Paid Business Networks

BNI (Business Network International): A well-known networking organization offering structured, business referral programs. Members pay to join a local chapter.

Chamber of Commerce: Local chambers often require membership fees but provide valuable networking opportunities with local businesses.

Vistage: A membership-based network providing coaching and mentorship for executives and business leaders.

EO (Entrepreneurs' Organization): A global business network for entrepreneurs offering peer-to-peer learning and connections.

YPO (Young Presidents' Organization): A global leadership community of chief executives with membership fees, offering learning and networking opportunities.

Each of these networks caters to different needs and scales of business, providing a range of options for networking, learning, and growing professionally.

In the UK there are two notable networks. The first one is FSB, The **Federation of Self Employed and Small Businesses.** The annual fee is reasonable and it comes with various member benefits. They offer a range of in person and online meetings. As a member you have access to hundreds of other members which means that by joining you can expand your network very quickly.

Another great UK based networking organization is **YBC, Your Business Community.** It is similar to FSB in that there are a range of member benefits and discounts. What I love about YBC is that they have a large showing at the annual Business Expo in London. They purchase a section of the Expo and allow their members to exhibit and a reduced fee. This gives small business owners access that they would not have without being a member of YBC.

Choosing The Right Paid Networking Group

BNI and the Chamber of Commerce, to name a couple. Each offered unique benefits. However, prior to the lockdown, as a side hustler, I found the commitment to regular face-to-face meetings challenging.

BNI, for instance, holds weekly meetings typically around 7:30am. These sessions are about connecting with other chapter members, sharing leads, and discussing your business. BNI's structure is geared towards quickly building a supportive network, but it's important to acknowledge that it has its pros and cons and may not suit every type of business. The disciplined schedule of BNI helps you manage your time efficiently and refine your business pitch. Each week, they feature an educational segment, and I had the opportunity to present for the Virtual Visionaries chapter in Houston, Texas. As the chapter name suggests, it's online, which brings its own set of advantages and challenges.

The online format is particularly beneficial if you have a non-geographic business, allowing for broader membership.

You're all welcome to visit this chapter. It's an enriching experience, and even if you don't join, you'll surely meet some fantastic people. But remember, it's crucial to do your homework. Talk to current members and ensure the group you're considering aligns with both your business needs and your availability.

Choosing the right network can substantially increase your sales by expanding your reach. After all, as the saying goes, "Your network is your net worth."

Networking's Best Kept Secret: WhatsApp For Business

WhatsApp for Business is a version of the popular messaging app WhatsApp, specifically designed for small and medium-sized businesses. This platform offers a variety of features tailored to meet the needs of businesses looking to communicate with their customers and network more effectively. Here's how it can be beneficial for networking:

Business Profile: WhatsApp for Business allows you to create a business profile with essential information like your business description, email address, store addresses, and website. This helps in establishing your brand's identity and makes it easier for customers and networking contacts to find information about your business.

Automated Messages: The app enables you to set up automated greetings, away messages, and quick replies. This feature is particularly useful for networking as it ensures that any new contacts or potential leads receive an immediate response, even when you're not available.

Labeling Contacts: You can organize your contacts with labels, making it easier to manage and follow up with networking connections. This helps in keeping your business contacts separate from personal contacts and allows for more efficient communication.

Broadcasting and Group Messaging: WhatsApp for Business allows you to send broadcast messages to a list of contacts and create group chats. This is useful for sharing updates, new products or services, and other relevant information with multiple networking contacts at once.

Catalogs and Product Showcases: For businesses that sell products, WhatsApp for Business lets you showcase your products or services in a catalog format within the app. This feature can be used to easily share your offerings with networking contacts.

Customer Support and Engagement: The app can be a powerful tool for customer support, allowing for quick, direct communication. Good customer service often leads to word-of-mouth referrals, indirectly aiding your networking efforts.

Analytics: WhatsApp for Business provides basic analytics, like the number of messages sent, delivered, read, and received. This data can help you understand how your networking and communication efforts are performing.

Business Networking For Startups and Side Hustlers

WhatsApp for Business can be an invaluable tool for networking, offering a familiar and user-friendly platform enhanced with features specifically designed for business communication and customer engagement. This functionality facilitates the maintenance and growth of professional relationships, sharing information about your business, and responding promptly to inquiries and opportunities.

Personally, I have utilized WhatsApp for Business to build communities that have significantly contributed to my business growth. As more interactions move online, small communities of business owners who have cultivated relationships over time will become increasingly valuable.

WhatsApp for Business, while not the only option, is one of the most underutilized platforms. In fact, statistics show that businesses using WhatsApp for communication see an average increase in customer engagement by 40%. Furthermore, a survey indicates that 70% of small businesses using messaging apps like WhatsApp report faster growth in customer base. So, give it a try and make sure to invite me to your group.

Networking Mindset Mastery: Overcoming Fear and Building Connections

One of the greatest barriers to effective networking is the widespread fear of public speaking, a challenge faced by many professionals. Surveys suggest that as many as 75% of individuals experience some degree of anxiety when speaking in public, fortunately I'm in the 25% who could talk your ear off. While I have explored various mindsets for startups and side hustlers in another book, this chapter will focus specifically on overcoming networking apprehensions.

Networking is not just about being extroverted or confident in public speaking as I am. It's about cultivating meaningful connections. Starting small and building up your confidence is key. For instance, while networking is crucial for business growth, it doesn't mean you need to start with a TED Talk. Begin with smaller, more manageable situations.

The rise of virtual networking, especially post-COVID, has added a new dimension to building connections. Business Network International (BNI), for example, has introduced virtual chapters since the pandemic. These virtual chapters offer a unique opportunity for those hesitant about in-person interactions. Being a BNI member and participating in these virtual chapters can be an excellent first step. It's a less intimidating environment where you can hone your networking skills. Moreover, you can choose a chapter that matches your comfort level.

Remember, effective networking starts with a mindset shift. It's about embracing the challenge and stepping outside your comfort zone. The regularity and structure of meetings in groups like BNI not only help in perfecting your pitch but also in becoming more organized and deliberate in your networking efforts. Networking, at its core, is about building relationships, and this often starts with changing your perspective on public speaking and interpersonal interactions.

Elevating Your Pitch: Communicating Your Value

Each year at the East London Business Expo, which I host, attendees can enhance their business presence through an elevator pitch. My extensive experience in hosting expos, including significant events in Houston and New York, has revealed a notable trend: many business owners, startups, and side hustlers are either intimidated by the idea of pitching or have horrible pitches.

The most impactful pitches are often those concise enough to be delivered within the first 30-45 seconds, yet many people waffle on. An elevator pitch is essentially a brief, compelling statement to spark interest in your business, ideally lasting no longer than an elevator ride.

Crafting this pitch involves several key steps: finding a pain point, providing a solution, succinctly explaining your business activities, highlighting your unique selling proposition, engaging with a relevant question, and ample practice to ensure a natural and confident delivery.

The essence of a successful pitch lies in its clarity, especially crucial in networking scenarios where attention spans are often limited. A well-crafted and concise pitch is more than just a tool for communication; it reflects your business acumen and demonstrates why others should take an interest in your business or service.

It's important to remember that many business owners overlook the fact that 'people buy from people'; therefore, avoid coming across as robotic or overly scripted. Don't take yourself too seriously, and strive to be unique. Say or do something that will truly capture people's attention.

An example of an elevator pitch

"Hi, I'm Anthony from Astor Business Centers, where we provide comprehensive business solutions for entrepreneurs and startups.

We specialize in helping people limited time and money. Our goal is to help you focus on growing your business. Astor Business Centers is your go-to partner for all your business needs.

Building Your Personal Brand in the Networking World

Okay, so I have to be upfront, I have a bias when it comes to this topic for two reasons. The first reason is that my wife runs a branding and design company, [Tiny Designs] (www.tinydesigns.co.uk).

We have offices in the US and one in London. She's amazing at what she does, so if you need affordable design and branding, she's your go-to. However, her being 'too affordable' tends to be a source of disagreement between us.

The second reason for my bias is that I used to have a graphic design business many moons ago, so branding and design are something that I know well.

When it comes to personal branding, I will draw from my experiences as a designer and company owner. I've noticed that too many people either take this aspect too seriously or not seriously enough. Those who take it too seriously delay their progress by weeks or even months trying to find the perfect shade of blue or the ideal font to represent them. This can be so frustrating. What I would say to these people is: if you have a horrible product, it doesn't matter how amazing your font and design are. On the other hand, some people don't even try to make their branding 'pop,' as we say in England.

Let me explain. You should take some time to think about the image you want to convey when you're out networking. The colors, fonts, and shapes you use in your marketing materials should be consistent and align with your overall brand and goals. Because we are specifically talking about personal branding for networking, you need to make yourself stand out for the right reasons. Not because you are obnoxious or loud, but because you bring something unique to the table.

Here's an inexpensive yet effective way to enhance your impact and branding in networking situations: create a magazine. Trust me, it works. I have produced 100 24-page magazines (physical magazines) at a cost of about $275, and it's worth every penny.

Here's how and why it works: When I go to networking events, I take about 10 copies with me, aiming to have no more than 10 meaningful conversations. When engaging with people, I DON'T talk about myself. I ask the other person open-ended questions that allow them space to talk about themselves. This way, I get to know them and figure out how I can add value to their lives.

If you're looking for a great printer, check out unitedgraphics.net. They are part of our BNI network in Houston and they are quick and reliable. Ask for Chuck and be sure to mention the book!

Because I'm not in a rush, I can spend time getting to know more about them. Inevitably, by the end of the conversation, they feel a bit guilty and ask about me. At this point, I share a few key things and try to steer the conversation back to them.

As the conversation naturally concludes, I offer them a copy of the magazine and explain that it contains information about who I am and what I do. The magazine is filled with useful information, hints, tips, life hacks, a list of people in my network, some articles I've written and QR codes to join my network or connect with me on LinkedIn.

Why does this work? Well, because I've focused on THEM, they feel valued.

Because I've given them something of value, they feel compelled to reciprocate. And because the magazine contains useful information and leads (through the classified listing in the middle), they perceive that I've added value. Not to mention, the people listed in the classifieds might gain a new customer. The result is that people remember me, and not just because my picture is on the cover, but because I did something very different. People have even started to call me 'the magazine guy.'

I would strongly advise giving this approach a try. It will have a significant impact on your personal branding and in expanding your network.

Actions for Branding

Specific: Define your unique value proposition (UVP) that sets you apart in your industry.

Measurable: Create a list of 3-5 key points that clearly articulate your UVP.

Achievable: Research your competitors and industry trends to ensure your UVP is competitive and compelling.

Relevant: Align your UVP with your networking goals and the interests of your target audience.

Time-bound: Complete your UVP and incorporate it into your networking materials within the next 30 days.

Specific: Establish a consistent brand image across all your digital platforms (LinkedIn, website, etc.).

Measurable: Update your profiles and websites with consistent branding elements (logo, color scheme, messaging).

Achievable: Work with a designer or use online tools to create or refine your branding elements.

Relevant: Ensure your brand image aligns with your professional goals and the perception you want to convey.

Time-bound: Implement the branding updates across all platforms within the next 45 days.

Specific: Engage with your network regularly by sharing valuable content.

Measurable: Post industry-related insights, articles, or tips at least twice a week.

Achievable: Schedule time each week to curate content or write your own posts.

Relevant: Share content that is beneficial to your network and reinforces your brand as a thought leader in your field.

Time-bound: Start this routine immediately and review engagement metrics after 60 days to adjust your strategy if needed.

Measuring Networking Success: KPIs and ROI

As I emphasize in all my books and training, 'what you measure, you can manage.' This principle highlights why having a clear strategy and KPIs (Key Performance Indicators) is crucial. In the personal branding section, I mentioned that my goal at networking events is to have meaningful conversations with no more than 10 people. This number is not arbitrary; it's a manageable maximum.

Statistically speaking, the average person can maintain a stable social relationship with only about 150 people (the Dunbar number), so focusing on a smaller subset ensures quality interactions. Beyond this, the likelihood of maintaining meaningful connections drops significantly.

One of my KPIs is the number of people I genuinely get to know at each event. This metric is straightforward to measure I ensure I collect contact details from each person and think of at least one person I can connect them with. Recently, I've started using a QR code linking directly to my LinkedIn page to facilitate immediate connections. Therefore, 'new connections on LinkedIn' becomes another measurable KPI.

Now, I have two specific, measurable, achievable, relevant, and time-bound (SMART) KPIs. From there, I can set follow-ups and track how many people I convert into network members, book downloads, or referrals. Your KPIs might differ based on your specific goals and that's perfectly okay.

The critical factor is having clear, quantifiable objectives aligned with your business aims. Networking is too pivotal and time-consuming to approach haphazardly.

While you might find some strategies in this book a bit cringe, they are effective. More importantly, they ensure you optimize your time and resources. Because most of my suggestions focus on people and relationship-building, they won't come off as insincere or robotic. Instead, you'll project a professional yet approachable vibe. Remember, people buy from people.

Since the topic of KPIs is on the table, it's the perfect opportunity to mention our CRM at WebsiteCasa Portal. Implementing a CRM from the outset of your business or side hustle is essential for scaling up efficiently, preventing data leakage, and automating processes to ensure exceptional service delivery. Even if you decide not to use our CRM, integrating your networking strategy into a CRM system is crucial. You can tailor a form specifically for networking purposes, a strategy detailed in various chapters throughout this book. If you haven't already adopted a CRM solution, now's the time to do so!"

Actions for KPI's and ROI

Specific: Track new connections made at each networking event.

Measurable: Aim to make and record details of at least 5 new meaningful connections per event.

Achievable: Use business cards, CRM systems, or digital tools to capture and organize contact information.

Relevant: Expanding your network is crucial for finding new opportunities and partnerships.

Time-bound: Review and update your new connections list after each networking event.

Specific: Follow up with new contacts within a set time frame after networking events.

Measurable: Send a personalized message or email to at least 80% of new contacts within 48 hours post-event.

Achievable: Prepare a template or key points to include in follow-up communications to streamline the process.

Relevant: Prompt follow-up is essential for nurturing relationships and maintaining the connection's momentum.

Time-bound: Set a reminder to complete follow-ups within 2 days after each event.

Specific: Evaluate the effectiveness of your networking efforts based on conversions.

Measurable: Set a target percentage for converting new contacts into active network members, clients, or referral sources.

Achievable: Use your CRM to track interactions, follow-ups, and conversions.

Relevant: Understanding your conversion rate is key to measuring the ROI of your networking activities.

Time-bound: Analyze your conversion rate and adjust your networking strategy every quarter.

Actions For Branding

Specific: Define your unique value proposition (UVP) that sets you apart in your industry.

Measurable: Create a list of 3-5 key points that clearly articulate your UVP.

Achievable: Research your competitors and industry trends to ensure your UVP is competitive and compelling.

Relevant: Align your UVP with your networking goals and the interests of your target audience.

Time-bound: Complete your UVP and incorporate it into your networking materials within the next 30 days.

Specific: Establish a consistent brand image across all your digital platforms (LinkedIn, website, etc.).

Measurable: Update your profiles and websites with consistent branding elements (logo, color scheme, messaging).

Achievable: Work with a designer or use online tools to create or refine your branding elements.

Relevant: Ensure your brand image aligns with your professional goals and the perception you want to convey.

Time-bound: Implement the branding updates across all platforms within the next 45 days.

Specific: Engage with your network regularly by sharing valuable content.

Measurable: Post industry-related insights, articles, or tips at least twice a week.

Achievable: Schedule time each week to curate content or write your own posts.

Relevant: Share content that is beneficial to your network and reinforces your brand as a thought leader in your field.

Time-bound: Start this routine immediately and review engagement metrics after 60 days to adjust your strategy if needed.

Strategic Networking: Choosing the Right Events and Platforms

When it comes to networking, not all events and platforms are created equal.

The key to strategic networking is selecting the right events and platforms that align with your specific business goals. It's about quality, not just quantity, especially if this is your side hustle. With limited time, you want to ensure that you are efficient.

A study by Eventbrite found that over 90% of organizers believe that event branding can have a significant impact on achieving event goals, emphasizing the importance of choosing the right events.

First, let's talk about choosing the right events. This isn't about filling your calendar with every business mixer under the sun. It's about targeting events where you will find like-minded people. Start by setting clear objectives: Are you looking to meet potential clients, partners, or mentors? Or are you aiming to boost your brand visibility? Understanding your goals will guide you in selecting events that are worth your time and energy.

Now, let's discuss conducting pre-event research. Check the list of speakers, attendees, and sponsors. Are there industry leaders you've been wanting to connect with? Companies that align with your values and interests? By identifying these key players beforehand, you can strategize your approach, prepare thoughtful questions, and even reach out for pre-event introductions via LinkedIn. In fact, according to LinkedIn, 80% of professionals consider networking important to career success.

But the work doesn't stop when the event ends; you must follow up, and as I have said several times, a CRM will help with this. Post-event follow-up is where the magic happens. It's what turns a casual handshake into a meaningful relationship. After the event, take the time to reach out to the connections you've made. Personalize your communication—refer back to specific conversations you had and express genuine interest in keeping the dialogue going. This is also the time to set up one-on-one meetings or offer resources that might be beneficial to your new contacts. Remember, the fortune is in the follow-up.

A study by the National Sales Executive Association found that 80% of sales require at least five follow-up calls after the meeting. Yes, 5 follow-ups. This number can be reduced if you made a meaningful connection when you first met by listening to them, suggesting someone that you can connect them with, giving them a magazine and connecting with them on LinkedIn. If you have done all those things, you might find that they reach out to you first.

In the digital age, online platforms are also a crucial part of your networking strategy. Whether it's LinkedIn, industry-specific forums, or even Twitter chats, virtual spaces offer invaluable opportunities to connect with like-minded professionals around the globe. One of the very best platforms for networking is Eventbrite. I not only list my events on Eventbrite, but I also find events to attend. Can I say on behalf of all event organizers, if you sign up for an event and then decide you are unable to attend, please cancel your ticket via Eventbrite. You will find some great events on the platform, many of them are free.

In my experience as an event coordinator, the show-up rate for free events on Eventbrite is about 40% (on the high end). The percentage increases as the price increases, but it is just good manners to let the organizer know how many people to expect, especially since many of these events are organized by small companies with limited budgets.

With that said, you could consider putting on your own events. It's a great way to increase your network, net worth, and database. If you do organize an event, be sure to invite me.

We'd love to meet you in person. We regularly do meetings, expos and conferences in the US and UK. For details about all of our events visit our Eventbrite page by scanning the QR code.

Actions for platforms

Specific: Identify and attend networking events that align with your industry and personal brand.

Measurable: Commit to attending at least two targeted networking events per month.

Achievable: Research events using platforms like Eventbrite, LinkedIn, and industry-specific forums. Use filters and keywords related to your industry to find suitable events.

Relevant: Attending these events will connect you with like-minded professionals, potential clients, and industry leaders, contributing to your business growth and personal brand enhancement.

Time-bound: Set a goal to identify and attend these events over the next six months, evaluating the effectiveness of each event in terms of connections made and opportunities identified.

Specific: Improve post-event follow-up to solidify new connections.

Measurable: Aim to follow up with 100% of the valuable contacts you make at each event within 48 hours.

Achievable: Use a CRM to organize contact information and set reminders for follow-ups. Prepare personalized follow-up messages or emails in advance to streamline the process.

Relevant: Effective follow-up is crucial for turning casual interactions into meaningful professional relationships and opportunities.

Time-bound: Implement this follow-up strategy consistently at each networking event you attend over the next three months.

Specific: Increase engagement and visibility on professional networking platforms.

Measurable: Aim to post valuable content related to your industry or expertise at least twice a week and increase your connections on platforms like LinkedIn by 15%.

Achievable: Allocate specific times each week for content creation and interaction. Engage with others' content by liking, commenting, and sharing.

Relevant: Active participation on professional networking platforms will enhance your online presence, establishing you as a thought leader in your field and attracting more networking opportunities.

Time-bound: Set a goal to achieve this level of engagement and connection growth over the next four months.

Here are a few ChatGPT Prompts that you might find useful.

Prompt: "Create a time-efficient networking plan for a side hustler who can only dedicate a few hours each week to networking. Include strategies for selecting high-impact events, maximizing limited time at events, and quick yet effective follow-up methods."

Use Case: This prompt is tailored for side hustlers who have to juggle their main job, their side hustle, and personal life. The response should provide a concise, actionable networking plan that maximizes their limited time, ensuring they attend only the most fruitful events and follow up effectively without overwhelming their schedule.

Prompt: "Develop a guide for leveraging free or low-cost online networking platforms and tools for startups with a limited budget. Include tips for creating a compelling online presence, engaging with potential clients or partners, and converting online interactions into real-world opportunities."

Use Case: Startups often operate with tight budgets, making expensive networking events or premium online platforms out of reach. This prompt aims to help them navigate free or low-cost digital resources effectively, ensuring they can still make meaningful connections and grow their network without significant financial investment.

Business Networking For Startups and Side Hustlers

Prompt: "Outline strategies for startups to create valuable, low-cost networking opportunities by hosting their own events or meetups. Include tips on event planning, budget management, and leveraging personal and digital networks to attract attendees."

Use Case: This prompt is perfect for startups or side hustlers looking to take a proactive approach to networking by creating their own events. Recognizing the constraints of a limited budget, the response will provide creative and cost-effective strategies for event planning, promotion, and execution, ensuring the host can establish a strong network base without incurring substantial costs.

Leveraging Storytelling in Your Networking Approach

Storytelling isn't just for bedtime stories with my daughter, Cadence. It's a powerful tool in the business world, one that can transform your networking approach and create lasting impressions. Indeed, researchers from Stanford found that stories are remembered up to 22 times more than facts alone. In most of my books, I include a short story relevant to the topic that shares my personal experiences. Hopefully, my stories are not only entertaining but also offer insights into my personality and values.

However, this approach is not suitable for every setting, as it could fall into what I consider one of the key 'no-no's' of networking: making the process all about you. But in the right setting, with the right audience, having a good story is a slam dunk. A well-told story can increase message persuasiveness by up to 30%, according to a study by the University of Minnesota.

Let me tell you, my wife, Leila, is an introvert, so if you are like her, you will probably find every suggestion in this book very challenging, but you need to push past that. Find your voice and tell your story. It will make you more human and allow you to connect on a deeper level. This approach doesn't just inform—it captivates. That's the power of storytelling. In fact, according to Harvard Business Review, stories can light up the brain's sensory cortex, allowing the listener to feel, hear, taste, or even smell the story, making the experience and the storyteller truly memorable.

Embrace storytelling in your networking efforts, and watch as you forge stronger, more meaningful connections. Remember, in a world full of data and information, stories are the golden thread that can weave true human connections.

Now, how can you leverage storytelling in your networking approach? Here's how to craft and deliver stories that resonate with your audience and make your pitches unforgettable:

Start with Your 'Why':

Every story has a beginning, and your business story starts with your 'why.' Why did you start your business? What problem are you passionate about solving? My 'why' was wanting more flexibility to spend time with Leila and Cadence. Let your 'why' be the emotional anchor of your story.

Add Personal Touches:

People connect with people, not faceless businesses. Share personal anecdotes or challenges you've overcome. When I talk about my journey, I mention late nights working while Cadence slept in the next room. It paints a picture and makes the story relatable.

Highlight the Transformation:

A good story has transformation—where your business or your clients were before your service and where they are now. Leila often shares before-and-after visuals of her design work, demonstrating the transformation her services bring about.

Make Your Audience the Hero:

In your networking conversations, frame your story in a way that your listener is the hero. How does your business or service elevate their status, solve their problems, or make their life easier? This approach makes your story directly relevant to your listener.

Keep It Simple and Authentic:

Resist the urge to embellish. Keep your story simple, clear, and authentic. People can tell when you're being genuine, and a sincere story is more impactful than an exaggerated tale.

Remember, in networking, your goal is to be memorable, to be the person they recall and want to connect with again. And just like Cadence remembers her favorite bedtime stories, your network will remember your compelling narratives. So, weave your experiences, your passion, and your victories into your conversations. That's storytelling in networking. That's how you make an impact.

Are you relational or transactional?

As we wind down, I want to share two more stories that are somewhat networking-related but are more about building meaningful relationships.

One of my closest and lifelong friends came about when I was an aspiring rapper. I got a record deal at age 19, thanks to KV, who was a dancer for Joeski Love (the guy that made the rap song Pee Wee's Dance), and my lifelong friend Sanielle. We mixed my first single called 'Games' at the Apollo recording studio in Harlem. The engineer was Fran Lover. While working on the project, we spoke, and he gave me some great feedback, not only on my song but also on how to develop as a rapper. He went above and beyond what he was paid to do. He didn't make it transactional; he made the process relational.

If you read Fran's discography, you will see that he has produced and worked with huge artists, including The Notorious BIG, so him working on my project was a step down in some ways. With that said, Fran and I are close to this day, which is why I am shouting him out. His approach aligns with studies showing that 85% of one's success in life comes from interpersonal skills, highlighting the importance of relational over transactional interactions.

Story 2: I won't even mention any names. When we opened our business office in Houston, Texas, in 2017, we needed a lot of print work done, including window signage and other big-ticket items. It just so happened that there was a printer within walking distance. So, for convenience, we paid them to do our window display, flyers, business cards, etc. Once we were up and running and offering graphic design, we started using them as our printer for all our in-house and customer printing. They are one of the most established bandit sign printers in Houston, so we started using them to print our bandit signs.

Within a few months, we were doing a considerable amount of business with them, so I approached the owner and asked her if she would consider referring her print clients to us if they inquired about websites, and I would pay her a commission since she did not offer a web design service. She said yes, but I would have to pay for the printing of the flyers.

Long story short, I printed about 500 flyers for her to display in her shop. Two months later, there were still about 495 flyers there, which was odd because this is a super busy shop. I did get two referrals, but it ended there. I eventually found an online printer and stopped using her because it was clear to me that our relationship was purely transactional.

I paid her for a service, and she did it. This is when I realized that I have to be deliberate and clear with the people I do business with. I am transactional with Walmart, Chick-fil-A, etc., but I want to be relational with mom-and-pop businesses. This means that we genuinely want to see each other succeed and will add value beyond the service being paid for. That is why I started the Startup and Side Hustlers WhatsApp group, and that is how the members operate. We are all there to make money, BUT we are relational and not just transactional.

Now I might be wrong, I'm not a millionaire business owner, so I am open to the fact that I might be going about things in the wrong way, but I do believe that being relational is the best way to be. Which are you?

This insight aligns with the finding that companies focusing on customer relationships over pure transactions have a 60% higher chance of closing a sale. So, are you transactional or relational? I believe that the latter paves the way for genuine connections and long-term success.

What Is A Prompt and How Can It Help Me Build My Network?

Prompt engineering is a creative and strategic process of formulating prompts or questions to elicit specific responses or actions, particularly in the context of AI and machine learning applications. In the realm of business networking, especially for startups and side hustlers with constraints on time and money, prompt engineering can be a powerful tool to garner insights, foster connections, and drive meaningful engagements.

Drawing inspiration from "Easy ChatGPT Prompts for Startups and Side Hustlers," here are five tailored prompts designed to enhance the networking strategies for budding entrepreneurs and side hustlers in the US and UK:

Identifying Value-Driven Connections:

- **Prompt:** "Considering the limited time and financial resources, and focusing specifically on [Your Business Type/Niche], how can I strategically identify and approach individuals or organizations within my industry that could offer the highest value or opportunity for collaboration? Could you guide me in developing a criteria-based approach to filter and prioritize my networking efforts effectively?"

- **Example Output:** "For a tech startup focusing on sustainable energy solutions, consider identifying key players in the renewable energy sector, such as industry experts, potential investors, or companies with a strong sustainability agenda. Utilize platforms like LinkedIn to filter contacts based on their involvement in green initiatives. Prioritize your networking efforts by targeting events or forums dedicated to sustainability in technology. Connect with these individuals by highlighting your commitment to renewable energy and how your startup aims to innovate in this space."

Maximizing Networking Events:

- **Prompt:** "Given the constraints on my schedule and budget, and considering I run a [Your Business Type/Niche], how can I make the most out of each networking event I attend? What are the key strategies for preparation, engagement, and follow-up that will ensure I build meaningful and lasting connections without overwhelming my resources?"

- **Example Output:** "As an owner of a small boutique digital marketing agency, maximize your time at networking events by preparing a list of attendees beforehand and identifying key individuals you want to connect with. Engage by asking insightful questions related to digital trends and offering brief insights into your unique strategies. Follow up with personalized messages, referencing specific points from your conversation and suggesting a one-on-one meeting to discuss potential collaborations."

Leveraging Digital Platforms for Networking:

- **Prompt:** "In a digital-first world, what are the most cost-effective online platforms for networking for someone in [Your Business Type/Niche], and how can I optimize my presence on these platforms to attract potential partners, mentors, or investors? What are the best practices for engaging with my network online to maintain visibility and relevance?"

- **Example Output:** "For a freelance graphic designer, platforms like Behance or Dribbble are cost-effective for showcasing your portfolio. Optimize your presence by regularly updating your projects, engaging with other designers' work, and contributing to community discussions. Use LinkedIn to publish articles on design trends or case studies of your projects to attract potential clients or collaborators, ensuring your content reflects your niche expertise in graphic design."

Crafting the Perfect Elevator Pitch:

- **Prompt:** "How can I create a compelling and concise elevator pitch that effectively communicates the essence of my [Your Business Type/Niche], resonates with potential collaborators, and fits within the time constraints of quick networking interactions?"

- **Example Output:** "For an eco-friendly apparel startup, your elevator pitch could be: 'At [Your Brand], we blend style with sustainability. We provide fashion-forward consumers with environmentally friendly clothing options, reducing the industry's carbon footprint without compromising on design or quality. Let's discuss how we can make fashion sustainable together.'"

Measuring Networking Success:

- **Prompt:** "What metrics or indicators should I focus on to assess the effectiveness of my networking efforts for my [Your Business Type/Niche]? How can I set realistic goals and track my progress in expanding my network, fostering relationships, and converting connections into tangible outcomes for my business?"

- **Example Output:** "For a consultant in the healthcare industry, measure networking success by tracking the number of new connections made with healthcare professionals, the frequency of follow-up interactions, and the conversion rate of these connections into consulting opportunities. Set goals for attending specific healthcare networking events each quarter, aim for a certain number of meaningful conversations at each, and track how many results in follow-up meetings or project collaborations.

Unlocking the Power of Networking for Startup and Side Hustlers

In "Networking for Startups and Side Hustlers," we talk about the art of networking, an essential skill for every startup and side hustle enthusiast. This isn't just a book; it's a practical step by step guide to networking.

Starting with the basics, we redefine networking as the art of building authentic relationships rather than a mere exchange of business cards. You'll learn the importance of active listening, finding common interests, and creating experiences that create meaningful relationships.

Timely follow-ups and CRM's are keys to successful networking. By employing SMART actions and strategic planning, you can navigate the crowds and stand out. This book emphasizes the art of adding value—sharing knowledge, resources, and opportunities to fortify connections, crafting a network that thrives on mutual benefit.

The journey progresses by guiding you through the selection of networking groups, including paid networks like BNI and the Chamber of Commerce, encouraging a careful choice that aligns with your business needs and personal availability.

As we conclude, the book reinforces the concept that networking is more than a business tactic; it's a vital life skill. Equipped with the knowledge and strategies within these pages, networking transforms into your superpower, capable of launching you to extraordinary heights of success.

The final chapters of the book are particularly useful:

Leveraging Storytelling: We explore the power of storytelling in networking, illustrating how sharing your journey and successes in a compelling narrative can captivate and connect with your audience on a deeper level. Real-life anecdotes about long-lasting friendships and business relationships showcase the lasting impact of authentic storytelling.

Measuring Success: This section is dedicated to measuring the ROI of your networking efforts. With practical insights and statistics, you learn how to quantify and assess the effectiveness of your networking, ensuring every handshake counts.

The book is filled with actionable steps:

Join a Structured Networking Group: Find and actively participate in a networking group that mirrors your business aspirations.

Leverage Technology: Harness AI tools like ChatGPT and CRM systems to enhance your networking activities, ensuring efficiency and effective relationship management.

Add Value Generously: Adopt a giving mindset, sharing resources and opportunities within your network, cultivating an ecosystem where support and generosity fuel collective success.

"Networking for Startups and Side Hustlers" is more than a read; it's a call to action. It encourages you to dream big, network intelligently, and let your entrepreneurial spirit take flight.

The world is ready for your brilliance, and it all begins with the connections you make. Your network truly is your net worth, and this book is your roadmap to networking mastery.

Have you ever considered writing a book? Networking is paramount, and events are foundational to business growth. As I mentioned earlier, it's beneficial to have something to give people at these events. Imagine the impact of offering a book you've authored.

Writing a book not only provides you with a tangible product to share but also enhances your credibility. In fact, a survey by the Author Marketing Institute found that 96% of authors saw a significant increase in their professional credibility after publishing a book.

Why Not Write A Book?

If you're interested in writing a book but unsure where to start, please feel free to contact me. I would be delighted to assist you. Regardless of your decision, putting your knowledge and expertise into a book is a valuable endeavor worth considering.

Don't let 'someday' become the thief of your time. Procrastination is the silent dream killer. Remember, every giant leap for mankind started with a small step on Earth. Starting a business is a lot of work but if you break it into smaller pieces, it is manageable.

Here's your mission. Pinpoint an upcoming networking event that speaks to your hustle. Commit to it. Write it down in your diary for the next month, not in pencil, but in the indelible ink of action. At this event, your target is to make three meaningful connections—no less. Reach out within 48 hours. This is how you stoke the fires of opportunity.

Now, let's talk habits. They're the unsung heroes behind every success story. Forming positive habits is like planting an orchard; they require regular tending, but oh, how sweet the fruits they bear! Every time you resist the siren call of procrastination and stick to your plan, you're watering those saplings.

So, put that note in your diary and circle it in red. Let it be a daily reminder that action is the antidote to inertia. Make it a habit, make it your truth. Today is your day, and now is your time. Because in the end, we only regret the chances we didn't take and the actions we put off. Your future self is counting on you, so let's get to it!

Closing But Let's Stay Connected

I'd love to connect with you and see how we can network. I'm available on LinkedIn and other social media platforms. We have US and UK Startup and Side Hustlers WhatsApp groups where you can meet people and share your product or service.

One of my favorite sayings is, "When the tide comes in, all boats rise." In my journey as both a business owner and an employee, I've learned that, as they say in BNI, "Givers gain." Networking is one of the best things you can do, and knowing how to do it effectively can change your life.

I'd love to hear your stories after reading this book, so please reach out and stay connected.

Whether you're a single parent managing a household and a business, a busy professional with entrepreneurial aspirations, or a student exploring the vast world of possibilities, the insights and tools in this book are designed to set you on a path of accelerated networking growth and success.

Don't talk about it, be about it!

Anthony Lindsay

Insights

Feel free to write down any after-reading this section

In 6 months from now I want to achieve...

- _____

- _____

- _____

- _____

- _____

Prompt for Customer Relationship Management (CRM):

Prompt: "Suggest strategies for implementing a CRM system in a small business, focusing on customer data organization, communication, and retention."

Use Case: For businesses aiming to improve their customer relationships, this prompt guides the implementation of a CRM system, enhancing customer communication and retention strategies.

Prompt for Networking Strategies:

Prompt: "Propose effective networking strategies for a startup owner, including both online and offline methods to expand their business contacts."

Use Case: Assists in expanding professional networks, crucial for business growth and opportunities.

Prompt for Branding and Identity:

Prompt: "Develop a branding strategy for a new [type of business], covering logo design, brand messaging, and identity guidelines."

To do list

Start to plan your goals based on the tips you learned

In 6 months from now I want to achieve...

☐ _____

☐ _____

☐ _____

☐ _____

☐ _____

Let's Connect

Now that you know a bit about me, I would appreciate the opportunity to connect on LinkedIn. I have an extensive network of serious business owners in both the US and the UK. It would be beneficial to include you in this network. When sending a connection request, please mention this book.

Do You Want To Write A Book?

Writing a book is a great way to share your knowledge. I want you to have every tool that I have access to. They are all listed on my book publishing page.

If you discover any other tools, be sure to share them with the Startup and Side Hustle community.

Here is our Book Publishing GPT.

If you're in the US please join our Startups and Side Hustlers Whatsapp group.

If you're in London or anywhere in the UK we have a group for you!

Need help getting started?

Are you a Startup or Side Hustler?

Do you need a website?

BUSINESSS
NETWORKING
FOR STARTUPS AND
SIDE HUSTLERS